DARTMOOR REFLECTIONS
David Mudd

BOSSINEY BOOKS

First published in 1993 by Bossiney Books, St Teath, Bodmin, Cornwall.

Typeset and printed by Penwell Ltd, Callington, Cornwall

ISBN 0 948158 90 5

ACKNOWLEDGEMENTS

Front and Back cover photographs from
MUSEUM of DARTMOOR LIFE, Okehampton

Front cover design: MAGGIE GINGER

LUSTLEIGH VILLAGE... An old postcard depicting more tranquil ▶
days, when an errand lad with his dog had time to pose on the bridge for a
photographer.

Lustleigh Village.

3

About the Author

Some twenty-five years ago, in the belief that everyone is capable of writing one book, David Mudd set pen to paper. Not only was there one book, but it has been followed by thirteen solo books and five collaborations with other writers on themes ranging from personalities to places; from facts to mysteries; and from history to the off-beat.

Having retired after 22 years as Member of Parliament for Falmouth and Camborne, he and his wife Diana now live just inside the Dartmoor National Park and this is his first book concerning what, as a staunch Cornishman, he regards as 'that Cornwall-in-waiting across the Tamar'.

David has been a newspaper, radio and television journalist and now has his own weekly news and current affairs programme on BBC Radio Cornwall.

Dartmoor – the Silent Witness

MEN may forget, but Dartmoor always remembers. Against the time-span of human experience, Dartmoor is ageless. Despite the repeated assaults of experts, writers, chroniclers, journalists, archaeologists, historians, painters and photographers, she has revealed as much of herself as she has wished, then, like her own famous mists, has swept back and hidden all she does not wish to be seen or recalled.

Were Dartmoor to be a reader of books rather than the famed setting of so many, she would no doubt allow herself the luxury of a smile or two when reading of herself ... the wry grin of a person totally misquoted in their own presence ... the tolerant shrug of one who has been represented ... the despairing gesture of one who has been misunderstood.

For, however excessive the defamation ... however inadequate the description, she remains voiceless and silent.

Or does she?

'The Fatherland of the Whole Family of Rains'

JUST because few people mention it nowadays, it doesn't mean that something didn't have more than a grain of truth at the time it occurred. And that's the hidden truth of Dartmoor – because it isn't there today doesn't mean that it wasn't there yesterday. What is inconceivable by modern challenge could still have been the norm centuries ago. The deepest bog of today might have been drought-parched one thousand years ago; and today's tallest story might have had an original – basic – foundation.

Take Sir Francis Drake, for instance. Because we live in age of militarism, we choose to believe that he outwitted the Spanish Armada by nautical brilliance and sound tactics.

But, for many years, there was a widespread belief that he enlisted the aid of the powers of darkness and actually drew strength from an alliance with the devil.

According to Dartmoor legend, the old sea dog was in close cahoots with Satan and, even before taking up bowls, used to entertain himself at night, if he was particularly bored, by driving a hearse pulled by black headless horses and accompanied by demons and yelping headless dogs, from Tavistock to Plymouth at the dead of night.

Worried about the possibility of being outnumbered by the Armada, he drove to Devil's Point – where there is a promontory jutting out into the Sound – for a chat with Old Nick.

His pal told him that if he cut pieces of wood and threw them into the sea, they would become as effective as gun-boats and thus increase his fire-power.

Sir Frank and the Prince of Darkness remained friends for sever-

8

al more years.

When Queen Elizabeth gave him Buckland Abbey, his only complaint was that there wasn't a barn. In three days one was up and ready.

One of his workers, unable to understand why things had moved so quickly on the first day, popped up a tree overnight to see if there was a night-shift involved. He later told his astonished colleagues: '*At midnight the devil came, driving several teams of oxen. As some of them were lazy, he plucked the tree in which I was concealed from the ground and used it as a goad. I lost my senses*'.

Exit one witness, and enter one fascinating fable.

Then there was the convict who escaped from Dartmoor Prison and became lost in a damp, cold fog. The one house he saw belonged to a man who was a writer of detective stories in the Sexton Blake series of paperback adventures.

Said the author: '*When I saw him, I wondered what Sexton Blake would have done. I suppose he'd have rushed in with a revolver, or waving a sword, and recaptured the man. I merely put on my hat, walked into Princetown, and asked the policeman to come back with me*'.

Exit one prisoner, but enter one more fascinating yarn.

The only thing is that this one, from the mid-1960s, happens to be totally true!

Then there's the mystery of the flowers on Kitty Jay's grave, near Hound Tor, Manaton.

Kitty killed herself after being wronged by the son of one of the local gentry. She was with child. The church decreed that maternity without marriage was a sin, so she found a convenient beam and a length of rope and, in the early 1800s, fitted rope to beam and rope to throat. Even then, the church showed no compassion and decreed that as she had taken her own life, she could not rest in consecrated soil. Her remains lie between two uncarved stones. The grave is regularly decorated with flowers ... but nobody sees them placed there.

And how about the rude shock that was awaiting the two midwinter callers at the *Warren House Inn*, between Postbridge and Moretonhampstead? Looking inside a large chest, they found the body of an elderly man.

He had died some time earlier and, until weather and conve-

PRINCETOWN… The melting snow seems to have marooned this village bus just outside the Prince of Wales pub.

nience made it possible to arrange a proper funeral, the resourceful landlord had laid the corpse in the chest, suitably preserved in vast quantities of salt.

Pubs formed a setting for other, less dignified, pursuits such as kicking and head-smashing. Moormen were very proud of the hardiness of their shins and – subject to a rule that no kick should be aimed above the knee – spent many hours kicking each other into submission.

Cudgelling, it was recorded, entailed the using of a thick stick 'the object to be attained by the player was the breaking of the opponent's head, the success of his praiseworthy efforts receiving the marked approval of the onlookers'.

Travellers might encounter pixies, or even drunken horses.

Dartmoor pixies had one or two rather admirable characteristics. If they 'borrowed' a child, it was merely so they could play with it.

10

If they liked someone, then they would often pop into the cottage overnight to do the dusting, the washing and the ironing.

They could, however, discourage would-be enemies by stopping their pleasant music and commencing 'a dreadful shriek'.

Of drunken ponies, let William Crossing tell a story: *'We had been loaned a Moorman's horse and were told we need give ourselves no concern about the homeward journey, for the animal "would carry beer". That he knew most of the houses at which his master was in the habit of obtaining that beverage we certainly found out to be the case, for on approaching a roadside inn at a smart trot, we were very nearly thrown by the animal darting to the doorway and coming to a dead stop'.*

There has never been a shortage of men and women adding to the vast treasury of books on Dartmoor and William Crossing was but one.

He lived, for a time, at Mary Tavy at the turn of the century. His great love of the history, the tradition and the legends of the Moor led to an almost endless series of books and articles. He was born in 1847, and died eighty-one years later. Regarded as one of the most energetic and accurate of researchers; fired by a love of Dartmoor; a determination to share his knowledge with all who would seek it; he had an absolute modesty that endeared him to all his readers and, which perhaps, kept him from producing the one gigantic catch-all book he once promised to write.

Alongside Crossing's books comes the work of the Rev Samuel Rowe, vicar of Crediton, historian and antiquarian, who wrote in less relaxed style. He lived from 1793 to 1853 and his major work, *A Perambulation of Dartmoor*, was intended *'with a view of rendering the numerous objects of interest, with which the great moorland district of the west abounds, more generally known and associated.*

Many of the legends and mysteries were committed to print by the Rev Sabine Baring-Gould who had an insatiable thirst for anything novel or off-beat.

He was born in 1834 and lived to be ninety. It was an action-packed incarnation. He travelled, he hunted, he preached, he wrote ... and he fathered many children.

His titles in print amounted to over one-hundred; his titles in flesh a mere five boys and nine girls! It was difficult to get to know them all and, on one occasion, at a children's party at Lew

THE REV SABINE BARING-GOULD, the squarson of Lewtrenchard.

Trenchard vicarage, he asked one little girl whose child she was. She looked up at him in disbelief.

'Why, yours, Papa', she said.

Three other distinctly more modern writers have made their own individualistic contributions to books on Dartmoor in three contrasting fields.

The only notable local writer of fiction to emerge in the twentieth century was A J Coles, a schoolmaster from Bovey Tracey, who took the name of one of Uncle Tom Cobley's compatriots – Jan Stewer – as the pen-name under which he wrote a long series of immensely funny dialect stories about life on Dartmoor. Sadly, whilst they delighted non-local men and women, the true Dartmoor villagers often found them patronising and too contrivedly rustic to have a comfortable ring of credibility about them.

Undoubtedly two of the best more recent men to present Dartmoor in a proper light have been Dr W G Hoskins and Vian Smith.

The thoroughness of Dr Hoskins was emphasised when an expert reviewer wrote of his book, *Devon*, published in 1954 that, although it was some six-hundred pages long: *'He leaves very little out, and his county patriotism is beyond doubt. He even finds room for a tribute to the achievements of the Devon Regiment'*.

The death of Vian Smith, at the early age of 50, in 1969, left between the covers of *Portrait of Dartmoor* the galling reality that Devon had lost one of the most able and promising of its modern portrayers. The grandson of Dartmoor hill-farmers, he foresook journalism to become a full-time writer.

He wrote with knowledge, with affection and with understanding in a way that could give history a fresh relevance. He portrayed Dartmoor *'not as a graveyard of three thousand years ago, nor as a National Park, but as a wilderness of heather and bracken where prides are deep and prejudices many; where the needs of several strata of society are perpetually in conflict and where the voice of Dartmoor man is too seldom heard'*.

Writing of Dartmoor and its people, he tackled the subject by breaking down barriers of pomposity and stilted language and painted places, characters and events with a warm, natural, skill that turned the black-and-white work of other writers and experts

Devon—Our County.

A TOAST.

Yer's gude luck to the land of old legend and song,
That have always stood up for the right agin wrong ;
To the land o' the West, where the sons o' the soil
Puts their hands to the plough and their backs to the toil.
    Gude Debenshur men, wherever you be,
    Ketch up your glasses and drenk 'long o' me.

Yer's gude luck to the land where the moors stretch out free,
And the hills wear a crown made o' mists from the sea ;
Where the wild red deer drenks to the stream in the goyal,
Where the maids be all fair, and the men be all loyal.
    Gude Debenshur men, wherever you be,
    Ketch up your glasses and drenk 'long o' me.

Yer's gude health to all they what calls Deb'nshur their home,
But have zaut out in zum vurrin parts vur to roam.
May they all make their fortins, and when work be past,
Come back to their own chimley's cornder to last.
    Gude Debenshur men, wherever you be,
    Ketch up your glasses and drenk 'long o' me.

Old and clean is her name, wide and free is her bounty ;
May God guide and keep her—Fair Devon, Our County.

JAN STEWER.

into a volume of vivid – but never brash – colour.

But Dartmoor is more a theatre of the natural than a backcloth for actors. It has vast contrasts in which the stark can be the beautiful, and the colourless can radiate vivid tones. It is a place in which the unexpected becomes the norm, and where accepted values have no place.

There's the spooky atmosphere of Wistman's Wood where even the shortest person gains delusions of height when bent almost double to pass between the stunted growth of age-old trees in this grove of dwarf oaks on the bank of the West Dart. Wistman's Wood can provide treacherous walking conditions due to the abundant growth of damp and slippery mosses which effectively hide gaps and deep holes between irregularly-placed rocks and boulders. And as if this isn't deterrent enough, the wood has a reputation as being the comfortable abode of a large number of snakes – not all of them harmless or friendly!

Spitchwick, on the other hand, is everything a beauty spot should be. It has ease of access; a fast-flowing, but clear, river to make it an oasis of coolness on even the hottest and dustiest of summer days; and the kind of 'all-things-to-all-kids' atmosphere that can, with a little imagination, turn it into a world of adventure to suit any explorer-games scenario from tracing the Nile to mastering the Amazon, or conquering the Rio Grande!

Few can resist the appeal of Becky (or Becka) falls, near Manaton.

As Vian Smith explains in his *Portrait of Dartmoor: 'There are huts for teas and souvenirs. But if you do not want them, you can get away among trees which give a green light in spring and summer, a bronze in autumn; belonging to the moors and contributing to its colours. I like to meander the paths and listen to the Becka in its haste to reach the river Bovey. Sometimes Becka becomes Becky Falls, but the middle syllable need bother none. It is merely demanded by Dartmoor speech, which likes to link two words with a middle syllable and cares little what it is'.*

Perhaps, though, Vian Smith was a little adrift in his belief, for it has been argued that the 'Beck' part of 'Becky' or 'Becka' has little to do with Dartmoor, but has more in common with the North of England word 'beck' commonly applied to a mountain rivulet.

If Dartmoor's roots run back to the days when great forests were but saplings and mighty torrents were but meandering streams, then Bellever must be one of the cradles of what the Moor was to become and what, hopefully, it will remain.

Forestry is not popular with everyone, yet around Postbridge and Bellever, the Forestry Commission has provided an economic crop as well as an attractive facility for tourists. Leave the official roads and walk on pine-needly carpets; smell the pine-laden air; hear and see the chortling streams; look at the delicate tracery of fern, of moss and of lychen; marvel at the new birth that puts tiny new shoots impudently beside stately and lofty tree ... and the timeless nature of Dartmoor is revealed in both its wonder of survival and its promise of continuation.

Purists will argue that the noble pine has no place on Dartmoor – and perhaps they are right. But who, having seen their gentle dignity and having paused beneath their shelter in driving rain or blistering heat would deny them their place any more than that the sycamore should be rejected, after years of providing much-needed building materials, fuel and shelter, just because it cannot claim an unbroken association with the dawn of time upon the Moor?

At least the rivers are not objects of controversy. Nobody imported them! They have been created to benefit dweller, worker, beast and tourist alike and give Dartmoor a rich series of aquatic arteries, each opening into a spot of breathtaking beauty at some stage of its journey from high-Moor.

Who can resist the tranquil beauty of Dartmeet where the East and West Dart meet, tumble, combine and make their way to Totnes?

For many years it has been a favourite picnic spot for visitors and, long before modern tourism, it was a point at which gipsy families gathered before moving on to local fairs and special markets.

In a steep fertile valley it provides a welcome respite from the severe and searching winds that sweep across the wild Moor on either side; a place where horses could be unhitched and watered; where many a fire could be lit; where many a heart would undergo the first joyous flutters of romance and love; and, nowadays, where

BECKY FALLS... The tumbling waters of Becky Falls still attract ▶
tourists.

DARTMEET... This postcard from the 1920s shows a surprisingly quiet and deserted beauty spot.

many a mile of film is exposed every week as cameras emulate the constant clicking of crickets and grasshoppers.

One of the ever-recorded subjects for photographers – bequeathed from the days when it was equally popular with artists and sketchers – is Haytor Rocks, complete with the remaining evidence of its unique tramroad.

Built in 1820, the tramway, consisting of granite setts laid lengthways and cut with a flange to anchor trucks to track, was used to carry granite from George Templer's quarry from Emsworthy Newtake, near Haytor, some eight-and-a-half miles to Ventiford, on the Stover canal. There it was loaded on to barges and taken to Teignmouth for transfer to larger ships for onward consignment.

Unlike other Dartmoor 'railways', the Haytor one depended on horsepower in its literal sense. Teams of eighteen strong horses were needed to haul a train of as many as one dozen wagons. Added to the weight of the load was granite, the horses had to overcome the friction caused by the fact that the trucks were not custom-built, but were merely road wagons adapted to run between the stone flanges that formed the 'rails'.

The tramway was in steady use from 1820 until the late 1860s with some of the stone carried being used in the building of London Bridge.

Haytor, itself, has been described differently by every writer who has attempted a word-portrait. Perhaps the Rev Samuel Rowe remains the nearest, despite the passage of almost two-hundred years, with: *'It rises from the brow of the hill with sombre grandeur in two distinct piles, and when viewed from the neighbourhood of Kingsteignton, and other adjacent lowlands, under the influence of a sullen and cloudy sky, presents a singularly accurate resemblance of a ruined castle, the massive keep of which is represented by the eastern pile'.*

If Dartmoor's physical features are legendary, then so are those of the elements – the mists, the fogs, the rain and the snows.

It has been described as the last great wilderness where bleak skies and brooding storms are never long-absent as if to wish to prove their absolute mastery and their ability to blot out a splendid view in a couple of minutes, or to turn a gentle stream into an ominous, dangerous, gushing torrent in a matter of hours. According to one early chronicler: *'It is the very fatherland of the whole family of*

HAYTOR... or as this postcard, one of the famous Frith series, has it – Heytor Rocks.

19

rains, from the mist to the waterspout'. It has, too, a knack of holding closely to winter when the surrounding lowlands are already well advanced into spring.

Modern expertise in search and rescue virtually guarantees that lives will no longer be lost on the Moor in even the severest of conditions, unlike the day in February 1853 when three soldiers of the 7th Royal Fuseliers perished in a blizzard whilst obeying orders to get from Plymouth to Princetown. The trio, two privates and a corporal, made their way through heavy snowdrifts before being forced to abandon their journey near the Devil's Bridge. They turned back on their tracks, but were soon lost in the snow. The corporal decided to press on to Princetown to get help.

Next day, searchers found his body only two hundred yards from safety, and the privates frozen to death some two miles further back.

In another tragedy, a farmworker came across the remains of a man who had lost his way in a fierce storm some six weeks earlier. Although the body of the man showed signs of starvation, *'it is said that his countenance was serene; his head rested on a small bundle of linen, and at his feet lay the remains of his faithful dog'*.

A resident of Postbridge, in November 1822, noticed a pauper passing-by on the road towards Chagford. His body was found four months later by some men tracking a fox on the open Moor a few miles further on.

A schoolmaster at Dartmoor Prison was another to lose his life in bad weather when he ignored the pleadings of friends at Moorshop, near Tavistock, to stay with them overnight. He told them that he could not stay as, due to the severity of the weather, his wife would fear that something dreadful had happened if he did not arrive home.

Similar disasters overtook a farmer from Tavy Cleave; a farmworker from Walkhampton; and at least one escaper from Dartmoor Prison itself.

Lightning has extracted its dues from the living, as have the Moor's rivers and streams. Indeed, the double-sided lethal-beauty of the Dart is enshrined in the couplet:

'River of Dart, oh! River of Dart,
Every year thou claimest a heart'.

Mind you, true Dartmoor people knew the secret of avoiding death altogether. By fastening the bolts and locks of the doors of a house, death could be kept away from a dying person. To be doubly certain, any mortally-ill person could be kept alive if they were laid on a bed made of chicken feathers or, indeed, the feathers of any wild bird.

Traditions may have fallen into disuse through the passage of time; superstition may be tolerated rather than exercised; death may have become a little less common at the hands of nature ... but the essential Dartmoor remains the same as ever.

She has been challenged, but never conquered; encroached-upon, but rarely violated; commercialised, but without loss of dignity; and although developed, has retained her identity.

EAST DART... The river cascades over rocks near Postbridge.

21

Tavistock

HISTORY is more generous to Tavistock than it is to Betsy Grimbal. While the town wins many glowing tributes for its attractiveness, its culture, its history and its commercial importance, poor Betsy is – at best – recorded as: 'a young woman, allegedly murdered in Tavistock abbey', or – at worst – as the victim of one of those strange and mysterious acts of violence in which: 'a man who was a villain cruelly slew a nun who was a fool'.

Of Betsy, no more … but of Tavistock, further detail.

Way back in 991, an abbey was founded there by brothers of the Benedictine Order. It became great and important both for religion and for its contribution to culture, boasting by 1525 a very early printing press. In 997 it had been burned to the ground by a group of raiding Danes who, led by Sweyn, had a right-rollicking trip up the Tamar, looting and destroying anything that caught their eye.

Not to be put off, the Benedictines built an even more splendid abbey and lived there in style until the days of Henry VIII, its walls built of Hurdwick stone, a granite hauled more than a mile from a quarry owned and worked by the brothers. Not only did they use the distinctive, durable, 'under-water-green' coloured granite for their own abbey, but they sold the stone to other parts of Devon for church-building. When much of modern-day Tavistock was built in the nineteenth century, Hurdwick stone was again in common use.

By the year 1105, Tavistock Abbey was already well on the way to becoming the largest and wealthiest in the South-West, the then abbot winning a charter for a weekly market followed by one to permit an annual three-day fair to celebrate Saint Rumon, from 29-

BETSY GRIMBAL'S TOWER...Showing the entrance and stone coffin.

31 August each year.

Within another fifty years, the abbey had detached some three hundred acres of its land to set up a community that was to become Tavistock. The abbot ruled the town with absolute authority and, in the early days of Henry VIII – while the corpulent copulating king was still an active Roman Catholic – London and Rome got together to elevate the abbot to bishop, independent of the diocesan bishop and even the archbishop, and to give him a peerage as well.

However, when Henry changed his ecumenical mind, separated from Rome and privatised the church and its lands, Tavistock Abbey was assessed as having a notional value of just £902 5s 7d (£902.27) and was handed-over at a knock-down price to the

▲ *THE IVY-CLAD TOWER… Betsy Grimbal's tower with its dense covering of ivy carefully trimmed around the windows – a photograph dating from the 1920s.*

▼ *THE PARISH CHURCH… Dedicated to St Eustachius.*

Parish Church, Tavistock.

Russell family. 'Knock-down' is a particularly appropriate description as the Russells did precisely that and reduced what had once been described as: *'an abbey that eclipsed every religious house in Devonshire in the excellent convenience and magnificent of its buildings'* to a pile of rubble, selling the various materials to any of their friends in the neighbourhood who wanted a new house or an extension.

What the Russells failed to destroy was further vandalised in Cromwell's day, when the Protector not only 'claimed' the town and its people in his campaign against King Charles, but also installed a sequence of hand-picked vicars into the life of the parish church – dedicated to St. Eustachius, and dating back to the 13th and 14th centuries, but subsequently updated and enlarged.

As a double-barrier against Tavistock becoming either Royalist or Catholic, Cromwell's authorities influenced the appointment of Thomas Larkham as vicar from 1643-1661. Larkham was found to be *'one of those interesting but unfortunate eclectics who find it impossible to side with any party and are therefore unpopular to all'*. He was *'a thoroughly goodly man, earnest and humble, and of a pleasant humour; but at the same time impulsive and over-sensitive, wanting in tact and somewhat bigoted'*. He was not a local man and had come to the area as chaplain to the parliamentary army, being invited to fill the vacancy for vicar that occurred while he was in the area.

Despite Larkham's admitted personality difficulties, he was regarded as a saint and a saviour when compared with Jasper Canne, who was vicar from 1673-1690. Where Larkham had been indecisive, inconsistent and humble, Canne followed strict puritanical codes of behaviour. If he could not have a new surplice, then he would wear none at all as it was unbecoming to his church and congregation to wear one that had been mended.

Summoned to Exeter for a rebuke by the bishop, he told his congregation that he was not minded to go as *'I do not care a straw or a rush for the bishop at Exeter, as I am bishop at Tavistock'*. On one occasion he asked parishioners to buy him a new pair of shoes.

It was said that he used church funds for his personal ends, accused of *'speaking profanely of the Bible; of using free criticism; of excusing attendance at Common Prayer to those who merely undertook to sit through his long and powerful sermons; and of pretending to be a poor, persecuted and distressed nonconformist minister for the excuse for begging in the streets of Bristol'.*

Tavistock and its incumbents were indeed vulnerable to extremes of chance, justifying the description of *'a town of mixed fortunes, at one time its vicar petitioning the parish for a pair of shoes, and at others its clothiers so wealthy and celebrated that Tavistock cloth was sought throughout the land as the best fabric of its kind'.*

If the earlier Russells were to be philistines, their descendants were to become local benefactors, providing an endless succession of improvements, extensions and facilities.

The Abbey Bridge was built in 1764 and widened in 1859-60.

Francis, 7th Duke of Bedford, did more in terms of providing civic buildings and public amenities for Tavistock than did any of the Russells over the previous three hundred years. He, certainly, (had he been born) would not have allowed Jacob Saunders, in 1725, to tear down one of the few remaining chunks of the abbey to make room for what his many enemies called the 'pompous dwelling house' that was to progress from house to pub and, eventually, to become what is now the *Bedford Hotel.*

Francis, the 7th Duke, remodelled the centre of the town in the 1840s. He erected the Guildhall, in 1848; laid out the magnificent Plymouth road; and even 'calmed' Saunders' vulgarity by giving the house exterior a style in keeping with his wish that the town centre should be of Gothic style.

His successor, the 8th Duke, decided to divest himself of the family's more flamboyant properties in Tavistock and offered all the civic and public buildings, markets, waterworks and pleasure grounds in his possession to the council at a 'first-refusal' price of £31,000 in 1910.

The offer was accepted with alacrity and gratitude.

One historian described Tavistock as *'that fruitful seed-plot of eminent men'.* It was no over-statement. There was, of course, Sir Francis Drake.

Although Plymouth would gladly claim him as one of their own, not only did the real Francis come from Tavistock (embarrassingly, nobody can pinpoint the exact place), but the statue on Plymouth Hoe is actually a copy of the original which graces Tavistock. It is the work of Joseph Boehm.

Other famous men from *'that fruitful seed-plot'* include Sir John

A very happy X mas to you! From Annie S Granger.

ABBEY BRIDGE... A scene little altered today – the weir at the bridge in the centre of Tavistock.

Glanville, Sir John Maynard and William Browne.

Glanville was the first solicitor ever to be appointed a judge. Maynard sat in both the Short and Long Parliaments and framed the impeachment of Thomas Strafford, former Keeper of the Rolls, for treason in 1641. The charges against Strafford were wild and imprecise. The prosecution could only find one witness. The evidence was questionable and were replied to *'with a fortitude, patience and ability that moved and alarmed his accusers'*. Although he won the moral and legal arguments, Strafford was still executed by an establishment that wanted copy-book trials and an endless supply of scapegoats.

Amongst the many beautiful memorials to be found in Tavistock parish church is one to Sir John Glanville. He is represented wearing the scarlet robes of a judge in the Court of Common Pleas. Kneeling beneath is the figure of his wife, Alice Skerret, dressed in farthingale and ruff. Beside her were the figures of their seven children. Now, sadly, some have disappeared.

Sending a post card from Tavistock to Putney, in 1933, a visitor

TAVISTOCK. TOWN HALL, GUILDHALL AND ABBEY GATEWAY.

CIVIC BUILDINGS... The Victorian town hall and Guildhall stand side by side with remnants of the old Abbey buildings.

who had obviously seen the tomb wrote: *'The little frock is charming. Don't you think she has said prayers for the two of 'em many a time? He is so placid'.*

One less religious and placid local lady was Lady Howard, daughter of Sir John Fitz. She was a mysterious character who managed to dispose of three wealthy husbands before she was wooed and won by Sir Richard Grenville. It is said that her dark and devious spirit can find no rest and that, almost every night for the last three centuries, she has turned into a hound and run to Okehampton and back between midnight and dawn, condemned to the task of bringing back one blade of grass per journey until either the grass is no more or her penance is done.

Tavistock has its memories, its successes, its greatness and its colour. Yet, perhaps it best lives up to some delicate but unsensational words of description as applied by the traveller, John Murray,

◄ *THE GLANVILLE MEMORIAL... The touching monument in Tavistock's parish church.*

29

SIR FRANCIS DRAKE... The town honoured its famous son with this fine statue.

in 1859: *'This thriving town will appear most delightfully situated to the stranger who has just descended from the naked Moor'.*

The words could not have been more aptly written by yet another famous son – William Browne, the Tavistock-born pastoral poet who was a contemporary of Spenser and Shakespeare, who 'got wealth and purchased an estate'.

Mires, Tors and Crosses

IF a walker on Dartmoor has strayed from the safe path and into water; if the feet are sinking into what seems to be a bottomless pit; and if the water – even in the heat of summer – has a frightening chill, it might seem rather academic to try to define whether the villain of the piece is a bog or a mire.

To William Crossing, however, it was important formally to state the difference.

'*A mire is distinct from a bog*', he wrote. '*The former is a swamp, generally the source of a stream, and is of such a character as to be in most cases impassable. By a bog is understood a stretch of wet, spongey, peat soil, and which though not to be ridden over, and in places not crossed, without exercise of care even by those on foot, yet presents no actual impediment to the latter*'.

So if the walker merely sinks – but survives – then it was a bog. Disappearance entirely means a Dartmoor mire.

There are many stories of death-by-mire. Some legends do, however, have a happier side. In one of these, a handcuffed prisoner was being driven across the Moor by a policeman. The convict, a local man, knew the Moor well and as they reached a certain point, he caused the cart in which they were travelling to tip over. He rushed towards an accommodating mire but his escort decided that it was better not to follow. Reaching the centre of the mire (which should, by Crossing's definition have been a bog rather than a mire), the prisoner turned to his former custodian and invited him to follow with the mocking warning: 'You can come in if you like. I know the way out, but you don't'. The escapee then trotted off to freedom.

The tors of Dartmoor are best described as being small hills usu-

Bowerman's Nose, A Druidical Idol,

ally capped by groups of picturesque rocks, although one romantic writer did coin the description of: *'Lofty tors which may often be discerned glittering with an Alpine scapular of snow, amidst surrounding verdure'.*

Although their names are often straightforward, others take their identities from a variety of unexplained sources. Bagga Tor, Pew Tor, Chat Tor, Nat Tor, Skat Tor and Yes Tor must all have had their names inspired by someone, some place or some thing ... but who, what, why and when?

Whatever their names, and wherever they occur, the very reason of the creation of the tors is common to them all – the weathering of the summit masses of the small hills, the hardness of the granite having combined with wind and weather to create shapes that can resemble animals and represent a bizarre but impressive stone individuality.

It seems that the combination of elements working against stone – the very ingredients that created them – is still at work and, having sculpted the shapes, is now destroying them. The coldness of winter creeps into the minute cracks where the rain and moisture of autumn lies and, as the water changes to ice, the surface of the rock is broken into tiny particles, thus wearing away the stone in a

BOWERMAN'S NOSE, left... and above, PEW TOR.

33

slow but relentless process. In addition to the tors – and they can be numbered in dozens – there are the more exclusive rock piles, of which there are but fourteen. For the most part, they have the same basic characteristics as tors, but carry such distinctive names as Bowerman's Nose, the Slipper Stones, the Dewerstone and Smear Ridge.

Bowerman's Nose is said to have been named after a bowerman, or builder, who lived nearby at Manaton. Certainly it does have an uncanny resemblance to a human profile.

Then there are the granite crosses and posts that marked the route of the safe paths across the Moor. In 1699, the authorities of Plymouth and Exeter agreed to spend £2 for erecting stones on Dartmoor to guide travellers along the safest and most direct route linking the two communities. Each cross or post had to be large enough to be clearly seen from its predecessor along the route; rugged enough not to be displaced by the elements; and clearly marked with town identities to reduce the chance of anyone wandering in circles and becoming hopelessly lost.

Another communications link was the network of Abbot's Ways linking the monks and monastic houses of Tavistock, Buckland, Buckfast and Plympton by a route that was so well-used that its traceable and compacted surface now gives the impression that it was paved rather than hardened by feet, wheels and hooves over many years.

WHITCHURCH DOWN… The Pixie's Cross, still to be seen, part of the network of guided ways for travellers.

34

Was Sherlock Holmes Right?

S HERLOCK Holmes was undoubtedly Britain's greatest fictional detective. He could see something important in the most insignificant of objects, be it a bell-pull, a saucer of milk or even a fleck of wool. In many ways he pre-dated forensic science itself.

The key to his miraculous skills of detection lay in his amazing powers of observation, none greater than on that day in 1993 when Doctor Watson found a photograph while browsing through Tavistock market.

It showed a police sergeant and three constables outside what was undoubtedly Tavistock police station.

'I know that, Holmes', said Watson, 'But when was it taken?'.

Holmes drew thoughtfully on his pipe for all of three seconds.

'I think I can narrow it down to a period of eighteen months in 1946-47', he said.

Noting the look of blank astonishment and disbelief on Watson's face, Holmes admitted 'there are, of course, at least six clues that lead me to that conclusion.

'The sergeant is only wearing stripes on his right arm. In Devon police they only adorned both arms from the 1950s onwards.

'I note that the four officers are all wearing their chinstraps. From 1945 onwards, straps were only worn during the winter time, so I believe this to have been a winter photograph.

'The third clue is that the second officer on the left is wearing his first aid badge. As these disappeared in the 1950s when open-necked tunics were introduced, this confirms the late 1940s as more than probable!

Watson was lost in amazement at the perception of his friend and mentor. 'But', he probed, 'the 1940s spanned a decade and you

have tried to narrow this to a specific eighteen months'.

'Be patient', said Holmes, 'I will explain further ... The officer with the first-aid badge wears his whistle chain attached to the top button of his tunic, whereas the others use the second button. This suggests that he is fresh from training school and has mingled with constables from other forces – such as Plymouth City, and Somerset – who used the top button.

'Then we come to the second constable on the right. He is showing what appears to be an inspector's pips. However, at the time this picture was taken – confirming my suggested dates – officers of Devon constabulary wore a button at the neck end of the epaulette, with the Divisional "letter", the officer's number and the constabulary crown leading down the shoulder'.

Watson could not believe that a simple snapshot could give so much information – even to so outstanding an observer and detective as Sherlock Holmes.

But the best was yet to come.

'Even you, my dear Watson', said the great detective, 'could not have failed to notice the medal ribbons. These would appear to be the 1939-45 war and campaign decorations. This would indicate that at least two of the officers, having served in the forces, had opted for "Class B Release" which granted accelerated demobilisation to any serviceman wishing to join the police or do some other job of great importance'.

Hooves and Horses

ACCORDING to the old song, the village smithy should usually stand 'beneath the spreading chestnut tree'.

In South Tawton, the smith worked under an elm tree that eventually fell foul of Dutch elm disease in the 1970s and stands no more.

Watched by two little girls, in starched aprons, and obligingly held by a young lad who, perhaps, had dreams of becoming a farrier himself one day, the grey cob – and the docked tail suggests it was very much a working horse – undergoes the horse-equivalent of a re-tread on one of its hooves.

The stony nature of Dartmoor soil made it necessary to fit replacement shoes every six or eight weeks. Despite the size of the nails, the roaring fire and the farrier's muscles, it was quite painless to the horse.

In 1915, farriers were beginning to consider travelling to the farms rather than await the arrival of the horse, as war-time agricultural production made it essential that no time should be wasted in the fields.

South Tawton is the most northern of the moorland border parishes, with a church dating back to the fifteenth century. For some reason, its pulpit only has three of the evangelists with St John the notable absentee. Whilst ancient worthies normally rest in ornate tombs, with head on cushion and feet on lion or greyhound, John Wykes, who died in 1592, rests his feet on a solid-looking duck!

At the churchyard gate of South Tawton is the remarkable and imposing Church House, a granite barn-like structure with medieval windows and a thatched roof. An eye-catching feature is

SOUTH TAWTON... A smith attends to a patient horse.

that the main door is on the second floor and approached by a double external staircase, whereas the downstairs has a sheltered – and modest – entrance alcoved by the impressive entrance to the floor above.

Clapper Bridges
and Two Bridges

ONE of Dartmoor's most famous and beautiful features is provided by those strange, practical, solid constructions, its famous clapper bridges.

They've been standing for upwards of seven hundred years and seem to mark the routes created by traders and travellers when would-be settlers followed the tin-streamers into the heart of the Moor.

They're robust, rugged, neatly-stacked and look as if they would have little difficulty in accommodating modern traffic – provided, of course, that cars, caravans and coaches had the ability (and the humility) to adopt a more slimline form.

The one standing so conveniently for photographers beside the road at Postbridge was probably used by trains of pack-horses in the thirteenth century, having been built by would-be farmers who needed a dry crossing. Unbelievably, it was almost destroyed in 1920 by a young man who, it is said, merely wanted to recycle the huge stones to stop his ducks from straying too far downstream.

After sixty years in its vandalised state, it was restored by the Duchy of Cornwall in 1880 and now stands at a proud height of virtually three metres above the bed of the river.

William Crossing writes of 'post-roads' crossing the Moor, and a map dating back to 1720 shows this particular bridge as being a 'Post stone bridge, 3 arches', suggesting that the name 'Postbridge' undoubtedly comes from this very basic description.

Until the 1800s, most of Devon's traffic was by pack-horse. A pack-horse train would have been very much like a commercial town on the move. The packs were slung from hooks attached to a

POSTBRIDGE… An ancient bridge spans the river – and a more modern sign advertises the Lydgate Hotel.

yoke or harness running down the back of the horse. In them would be brushwood, roofing materials, lime, coal, corn or hay. The packs would be so wide that it seemed impossible that two beasts could pass one another on the narrow tracks or crossings. Loads too heavy to be placed on the backs of the horses were put on rough sleighs called 'truckamucks'. This grand-sounding title merely disguised a more simple construction that was no more than two young trees with their tops fastened together to provide a 'saddle' over the horse's back, and with the rooted ends dragging along the ground.

There is another surviving clapper bridge at Two Bridges.

One, at Ashburton, was washed away in August 1826 when the river rose to a great height. Entrapped in the melee of seething water was a huge tree which, seemingly, behaved rather like the agitator in a modern washing machine and gradually smashed down the arches of the bridge.

Just set back from the road, at Two Bridges, is what is now known as the *Two Bridges Hotel.*

It dates back to the days of Sir Francis Buller, a man who will ever be remembered for his attempts to turn Dartmoor into an economic success. In the late 1700s he lived at Prince Hall and, by enclosing two thousand acres of moorland, set a pattern of successful farming to bring stability to the area.

It was said that he found 'pleasure and amusement' in his good work and that his name would 'ever be remembered among those who have endeavoured to introduce cultivation into that wild region'.

It was Sir Francis who built the first inn at Two Bridges and had it marked with his crest – a Saracen's Head.

Sir Francis gathered, according to William Crossing, *'quite a little colony of workers about him, to whom he was most kind, and ever ready with his advice. His hospitalities were always open to the stranger, and the house was the constant resort of men experienced in the science of agriculture, from all parts of the country'*.

In the summer of 1832, Tom Satterley worked as an ostler at the *Two Bridges Inn*. He was to marry a fascinating local lady named Sally. Sally, for her part, was as good a man as the rest of them. She could shoe a horse; cut peat, mow with a scythe; and drive a pack-

The Two Bridges, Dartmoor

Valentine's Series

TWO BRIDGES… A note in faded ink on the back of this postcard tells us this is where the tavern called the Ring o' Bells stood, mentioned in The River.

JOLLY COT… Reputedly the last house on Dartmoor to be constructed under an old commons tradition.

horse whenever the need arose, having been apprenticed, at the age of seven, alongside local lads into the skills of farming.

Tom and Sally decided that Midsummer Day would be the best day for their wedding. Sally, being Sally, knew what she was doing.

According to custom on the Moor, if anyone could build a house on common land, starting from scratch at dawn, and have it completed by nightfall, with roof intact and fire burning, then no person or court had the right to evict them and they were entitled to it forever.

On Midsummer Day 1832, Sally and Tom were up before dawn and gathering materials – granite for the walls, wood for the door and bracken for the roof. They chose Midsummer Day for two reasons. Firstly, it was the longest possible working day; and secondly because they knew that the local farmers would be heading off to Holne for celebrations that would include ram roasting and would keep them away from the site, just beyond Huccaby Bridge, that the couple had selected.

The absence of the farmers was critical. They argued that there were enough houses on the Moor already, without people adding to the pressures on rights to graze; and the right to cut bracken for bedding and peat for burning. As each new building erected under the ancient tradition only encouraged other dwellers, farmers would do all they could to hamper work and make it virtually impossible to meet the 'complete your house in a day' deadline.

As the farmers made their way to Holne, Tom and Sally were joined by their families and friends. By evening the walls were finished at a height of just under two metres. The thatch was created by bundles of furze and, with a few hours to go, the first wisp of smoke ventured forth – out of the door – as the chimney, like the second floor, had to wait for another day.

However, they had fulfilled the requirements and lived there until, some years after Tom's death, Sally died in 1901 and was accorded the traditional Dartmoor walking funeral in which relays of men carried her coffin across the Moor to Widecombe for burial. Her casket carried the last words she uttered: 'Nothing in my hands I bring, simply to the Cross I cling.'

They carried Sally's coffin, with women mourners following the teams of bearers. Every so often they put it down, and sang psalms and hymns before lifting their precious burden for the next stage of the sad journey.

Although given the full Dartmoor funeral honours, Sally Satterley's initials are not amongst those visible on the side of the path leading upwards from Dartmeet to Widecombe. There are, at this point, two adjoining blocks of granite known as 'the Coffin Stone'. Upon this, the body was rested whilst the walking mourners gathered their own strength for what was still to be a long walk. On the stone it was customary to pause and carve the initials of the deceased person. Although five sets of initials can still be deciphered, those of Sally are not amongst them.

The *Two Bridges Hotel* was to retain Sir Frank Buller's links with agriculture in a colourful way.

It became the setting for the annual Duchy of Cornwall Rent Audit Lunch when in recognition of the payment of all outstanding dues the Duchy of Cornwall entered a new farming year each autumn by entertaining its tenants to lunch. They were, after a huge lunch, given glasses of port, tobacco and long stemmed churchwarden's pipes made of clay. With glasses and pipes

DARTMEET… Carefully balanced granite stones allow a dry-footed crossing.

charged, they then toasted 'The Duke of Cornwall' and were told of further development plans and philosophies for the Duchy lands on Dartmoor for the coming year.

Nowadays, the *Two Bridges Hotel* has two other claims to fame.

Firstly, its llamas – introduced in 1992 by the owner, Philip Davies. Although these strange animals owe their origin to the exotic heights of the Andes, they seem content to live on the Moor. However, should they breed widely and then go into decline, it would be interesting to know how a future historian will seek to explain their fossilised bones.

Secondly, the fame of the *Two Bridges Hotel* also lies with its Devonshire cream teas. These are not for the timid or those who can't look a decent treat in the face. It's as if Philip Davies and his team have decided that if any army can march on its stomach, then tourists and trippers must march on scones, jam and cream served in massive portions.

But, a Dartmoor health warning states on the advertisements, 'Our cream teas can prove addictive'.

They do.

Craim 'n' Chaise 'n' Zider 'n' Dumplins

CALORIES had probably not become a topic of health obsession when 'Auntie Elsie' wrote to her nephew, Master B Baldry, from Yelverton, on 23 December 1909.

To his home at Easton Cottage, Quarry Street, Stonehouse, Plymouth, she sent a postcard warning of her intended Christmas visit. On the back was the message: 'I wonder if this dumpling was made at a farm near here. It will just make the farmer fat'.

There was no need for someone living at Yelverton to translate 'To wish you all you wish yourself this Christmas-time' from the quaint dialect on the front of the card, but Auntie Elsie clearly thought that 'Waant ee'ave bit o' thicky Devenzhur Dumplin? It be a fus' raate wan' as justifying an interpreter's note to the effect that it was inviting the reader to have 'a bit of this Devonshire Dumpling' and confirming that it was 'a first rate one'.

The dumpling was but one of the delicacies associated with the Moor, alongside cheese, cream, cider and good old-fashioned crusty bread.

Indeed, translated into post card Devonese, 'here, have a hunk of bread and cheese, and a glass of Devonshire cider, could become – with liberties taken – 'yer, 'ave a hunk o' braid 'n' chaise, an' a glass o' Devnzhur zider'.

That this strange tongue was taken as authentic was confirmed by 'B' who passed them to a friend in Horsham as 'a bit of broad Devonshire' adding: 'the braid 'n' chaizes and zider are alright after a good walk'.

Although many of the Dartmoor cheeses were serviceable, strong and generally unremarkable, this could not be said of the palate-

45

YER,'AVE A HUNK'O BRAID'N CHAISE, AN'A GLASS'O DEVENZHUR ZIDER.

DEVON FARE… The message on the back of this card says it is 'all right after a good walk.'

teasing Devon Garland, a semi-soft cheese 'sandwich' on either side of a band of fine herbs.

Devonshire cream was – and remains – a great favourite amongst locals and visitors alike.

Cream was certainly commonplace by the early fourteenth century. With an absence of any effective cooling process, fresh milk would soon curdle in hot weather or if there was thunder about. It was discovered – it is claimed by the monks of Tavistock Abbey in the late 1300s – that the life of milk could be extended merely by boiling it.

Further experimentation showed that if the milk was taken beyond mere boiling, it could be scalded until it became cream. In a further process, the cream could then become the basis of butter if the cold cream was agitated.

Although much of today's Devonshire cream is commercially manufactured, some of it is still made in the kitchens of farmhouses or country cottages.

The milk is strained into shallow dishes and allowed to stand for about twelve hours. It is 'scalded' by being heated to a high temperature and held for about forty minutes before being allowed to cool. Then, after a further period of standing, the yellowy and wrinkled top is gently skimmed-off, taking with it the familiar grainy, rich texture that elevates it from the runny milky fluid called 'cream' elsewhere.

Massive demand from local, national and international sales have now largely transferred manufacture to vast creameries where automatic separators and thermostatically-controlled technology are a cost-effective substitute to traditional cream making.

In the old days of deeply superstitious Dartmoor, it was darkly hinted that any wife or daughter who could not get the milk to turn into cream failed because she walked in the darkness of the shadow of evil!

But it was the dumpling that was Devonshire's most famous dish.

Its story appeared in some detail on a post card a century ago: *'The hunger of a nobleman is responsible for the fame of these dumplings. His Lordship was hungry (very hungry we would think) & he cast his famished eyes about the village through which he was passing for the usual inn.*

'Devonshire Dumplings'
The hunger of a nobleman is responsible for the fame of these dumplings. His Lordship was hungry (very hungry we should think) & he cast his famished eye about the village through which he was passing, for the usual inn 'twas missing. Well he must try a farm house. But the good lady protested that she had no bread. "Would his Lordship try some dumplings"? "Needs must when the devil drives". So his Lordship tried the dumplings. No sooner had the first morsel passed his lips than he recognised their quality & dumpling after dumpling passed down his loose gorget with a rapidity which spoke volumes for their goodness The astonishment of the dame was great & the villagers lost not the opportunity of seeing the Animal feed.

DEVONSHIRE DUMPLINGS… The card depicting this story was sent from Skegness to Grimsby in 1908.

47

It was missing. Well, he must try a farmhouse. But the good lady protested that she had no bread. "Would his Lordship try some dumplings"? "Needs must when the devil drives". So his Lordship tried the dumplings. No sooner had the first morsel passed his lips than he recognised their quality & dumpling after dumpling passed down his loose gorget with a rapidity which spoke volumes of their goodness. The astonishment of the dame was great and the villagers lost not the opportunity of seeing the Animal feed'.

One of the essential ingredients of the true dumpling is suet – the hard fat to be found round the kidneys of cattle and sheep – a commodity in great supply on and from Dartmoor. Perhaps, therefore, it was a case of taking coals to Newcastle when the suet makers, Atora, sent their publicity waggon to Tavistock on April 1 1926, drawn by two beasts of such magnificence that even farmers marvelled in their excellence.

Cider, or 'scrumpy' is the nectar of the gods and mortals of Dartmoor alike.

Although nowadays it's regarded as pretty innocuous, except when drunk to excess by fools and the ignorant, it once played an important part in the economy of Dartmoor employment as its pro-

CHRISTMAS CARD… Master Baldry in Stonehouse got this card from his Aunt Elsie promising him a visit on Christmas Day 1909.

TAVISTOCK 1926... These splendid beasts drew a crowd of admiring onlookers on a spring day in Duke Street.

vision was offered, and accepted, as part of a labourer's pay.

At times of heavy or hot work, kegs were set up at strategic points on hedges or boundaries and the labourer was expected to dig, cut or reap his way from point of refreshment to point of further refreshment. The scrumpy was often made on the farm itself and was thus a cheap product. Sadly, its roughness, its impurities or its sheer headiness could lead to illness or addiction as a man undertaking heavy exertion might drink as much as sixteen pints a day.

It was said that the menace to home and health became so great and so real that the local clergy would often lead prayers for the failure of the cider apple crop in the early 1800s.

They Went to Widecombe

IF OLD Uncle Tom Cobley went anywhere with his rollicking crew, squeezed upon the back of Tom Pearce's geriatric, over-loaded and overstretched equine all those years ago, it wasn't Widecombe.

Although the evergreen Devonshire song has kept Widecombe Fair amongst Britain's best-known country events, there is nothing to verify the claim that any event has ever taken place there that could justify the boast of antiquity.

Despite this, Widecombe has established itself as the setting for a much-attended September fair where, amongst the roundabouts, the rides, the stalls and the sideshows, there has been a tradition of trading in cattle, sheep and Dartmoor ponies.

Indeed, when William Crossing was writing *One Hundred Years on Dartmoor* at the end of the nineteenth century the whole story of Uncle Tom Cobley, Bill Brewer, Jan Stewer, Peter Gurney, Peter Davey, Dan'l Whiddon and Harry Hawk was only just being popu-larised through the writings of the Reverend Sabine Baring Gould, of Lewtranchard, based on a folk-song that had been around for a few years and would, incidentally, become the 'signature tune' of men of the Devonshire Regiment when they went to fight the Boers, South Africa, in 1899.

Vian Smith, in *Portrait of Dartmoor*, explains: '*The song about Widecombe Fair is well known. It tells how Tom Cobley and a group of friends borrowed a mare and came across the moor to Widecombe. This mare was grey, meaning white; for no Dartmoor horse is called white. The colour is essential to the story because in the closing verses, the mare dies and becomes a ghost; a white apparition to haunt the lonely places. The*

Widdecombe Fair

Tom Pearce, Tom Pearce, lend me your grey mare,
   All along, down along, out along lee.
For I want for to go to Widdecombe Fair,
   chorus Wi' Bill Brewer, Jan Stewer, Peter Gurney,
      Peter Davy, Dan'l Whiddon, Harry Hawk,
      Old Uncle Tom Cobleigh and all,
      Old Uncle Tom Cobleigh and all.

And when shall I see again my grey mare?
   All along, down along, out along lee.
By Friday soon or Saturday noon,
      Wi' Bill Brewer, Jan Stewer, etc.

Then Friday came and Saturday noon,
   All along, down along, out along lee.
Tom Pearce's old mare hath not trotted home,
      Wi' Bill Brewer, Jan Stewer, etc.

So Tom Pearce he got up to the top of the hill,
   All along, down along, out along lee.
And he seed his old mare a-making her will,
      Wi' Bill Brewer, Jan Stewer, etc.

So Tom Pearce's old mare, her took sick and died.
   All along, down along, out along lee.
And Tom he sat down on a stone and he cried,
      Wi' Bill Brewer, Jan Stewer, etc.

But this isn't the end of this shocking affair,
   All along, down along, out along lee.
Nor, though they be dead, of the horrid career -
      Of Bill Brewer, Jan Stewer, etc.

When the wind whistles cold on the moor of a night,
   All along, down along, out along lee.
Tom Pearce's old mare doth appear gastly white,
      Wi' Bill Brewer, Jan Stewer, etc.

And all the long night be heard skirling and groans,
   All along, down along, out along lee.
From Tom Pearce's old mare in her rattling bones,
      And From Bill Brewer, Jan Stewer, Peter Gurney,
      Peter Davy, Dan'l Whiddon, Harry Hawk,
      Old Uncle Tom Cobleigh and all,
      Old Uncle Tom Cobleigh and all

UNCLE TOM COBLEY AND THE GREY MARE

real purpose of the song was not to celebrate Widecombe Fair but to per-
petuate an old superstition, not confined to Dartmoor or English folk-lore,
that there is a ghost somewhere in the night'.

So there you have it!

But there actually was an Uncle Tom Cobley. He lived in the
eighteenth century, died in 1794, aged 96, and lies buried in the
churchyard at Spreyton.

There was, too, a Bill Brewer, a Jan Stewer, a Peter Gurney, a
Peter Davey, a Dan'l Whiddon and a Harry Hawk. They all came
from Sticklepath and would have travelled about twelve miles to
attend the sale of animals, perhaps pausing for a meal and a drink
before going home. Perhaps they did see a ghost one night.

However, their popularised contribution to the folklore of
Dartmoor was ridiculed by no less an authority than the Dartmoor
National Park Committee which found Widecombe Fair to be
'quite alien to the nature and spirit of Dartmoor'.

But, to quote Vian Smith again: '*The assumption seems to be that*
Widecombe Fair is not true to its history or to its original purpose. In a
way it is not; for although there are competitive classes for sheep and
ponies, the fair is no longer an important market. But in another way it is.
The second half of the fair was always the bringing together of many people

in a mood of holiday; and socially this half was always more popular than the first. It was the mood of holiday which Uncle Tom and his friends were seeking when they came across the moor; it was this mood which made Widecombe Fair the day to remember in a frugal year; and it is this mood which the modern mood preserves. Its din and candy floss and try-your-luck have developed out of the dumb-shows and organ boys of the past'.

So, even if Widecombe Fair wasn't well-founded to the satisfaction of the historian-purists, and isn't acceptable to the custodians of our modern culture, it still has a unique place in the folklore of Dartmoor.

Widecombe, itself, has a positive claim to recognition.

Its immensity of 11,000 acres, of which almost one half is wild moorland, warrants statistical recognition as a parish. Its roots date back to the days of the Bronze Age and its loftier heights – 1697 feet up, at Hameldown – were topped by a beacon to give warning of the approach of possible danger in Elizabethan times.

Its church, St Pancras, may share its name with a London railway station, but in age it is many times its senior, dating back to the fourteenth century, with embellishments and enlargements over the next two hundred years to establish it firmly as the popularly-regarded 'cathedral of the Moor'. Its tower is classified as one of

the finest throughout the West of England, combining grace with strength and character.

One awful afternoon – and the word 'awful' is the only appropriate one – in October 1638, the church was struck by lightning whilst a service was in progress.

As the storm raged outside, worshippers asked the vicar, the Reverend George Lyde, if it would be safe to leave.

He told them: 'It is better to make an end with prayer, for it were better to die here than in another place'.

The congregation stayed where they were. Lightning struck the tower, hurling huge boulders in all directions. Four people were killed and many were seriously injured. Counting dead, badly injured and those with minor injuries, the toll that afternoon involved sixty-six people.

It was said that the devastation was clearly the work of the Devil who had been seen, earlier that day, riding recklessly through Poundsgate on a black horse breathing fire.

Some suggested that the disaster showed the displeasure of God that Widecombe, despite its importance, always shared a split incumbency with another church, thus reducing the number and frequency of services. One minister was rector of Shaldon as well as of Widecombe. To treat both livings fairly, he lived in neither parish, but at Teignmouth!

Mind you, many of the worshippers were not very regular either. In the days of Bishop Bronescombe, in 1260, there were only two churches in the sector of the Moor – Lydford and Widecombe. This was so inconvenient to would-be attenders that, under a special dispensation, they were only expected to attend Widecombe three times a year, taking their tithe of lambs with them. Lydford was the centre of attendance for the payment of other tithes.

Widecombe has a proud and interesting heritage and most certainly does not justify the views expressed in an official guide book that 'The intelligent visitor will not wish to linger in it today' or that, on the day of Widecombe Fair, 'All the roads leading to it are best avoided'.

Widdecombe-in-the-Moor Church

The Harvest Tea

Harvest time meant work for everyone ... but a chance to have a family get-together in mid-afternoon. As Joe Endacott and his workers paused in the fields of Clannaborough farm, Throwleigh, in 1905, they were joined by the whole family – as well as the family dog – to face the photographic lens. There being

ladies present, the gentlemen kept their hats on, although one of
them so forgot himself as to take a few contented puffs at his pipe.

In 1993, three of the young ladies in the picture were still alive
although well into their nineties. Marion, on the left, and Ida, on
the right, did not marry. Suzie, lying beside Ida, became Mrs Eick.

Dartmoor Coal and other Industries

WHEN 'Frank' wrote to Mr W A Finch, at 98 Kings Cross Road, London W6, on 14 August 1912 – from Sticklepath – he had 'spent a good time at Torquay and Paignton and found Chelston people all right'. He was on his way to the show at Belstone but seemed totally unaware of the importance of peat, as featured on his post card, to the economy of Dartmoor and, indeed, the wellbeing of its people.

The right to cut peat was the inalienable privilege claimed by all true Dartmoor dwellers. It had been cut and used as fuel, and known as 'Dartmoor coal', from medieval days.

It is a source of fuel lying up to almost two metres deep in places, and caused by a strange climatic fault under which high rainfall and low temperatures prevent decaying growth from becoming pure humus, the spongey nature of the composition holding water and releasing it slowly.

Peat was traditionally cut at the end of July and then spread out to dry until, around October, colder weather made it both needed for burning as well as dry enough for use.

Digging peat was both heavy and damp.

It was cut in what were known as 'journeys'. A 'journey' was a row about fifteen metres long, three turves wide and a depth varying from one-and-a-half to two metres. Each brick was cut to about half a metre long.

According to one of the last commercial peat cutters: *'Drying the turves out was the problem. It was damp all the time up there. Most of the time was working in rain or mist and the peat would never dry out proper. They tried pressing out the water, but it crushed the peat as well. It was a tough life, but like I said, you did it because there wasn't no other.*

58

CUTTING TURF TIES (PEAT) DARTMOOR 1913

'There were six of us worked out of Bridestowe up to the peat works between Amicombe Hill and Great Links Tor. About six miles it was, 'and-some in the summer with the sun climbing over Amicombe, but bitter in the winter with the rain driving in your face. We'd arrive at the works soaked and work all day in that state. Most of the work was outside and there was not a tree for to shelter'.

Not only was peat the basic fuel of the Moor farmer, but it was also extensively used in the towns and villages on the fringes of Dartmoor, it being commonplace to see strings of pack-horses making their way to various communities, rather like the pack-horse trains associated with smuggling in neighbouring Cornwall. One elderly woman spoke of the eagerness with which her arrival with peat was awaited; how people crowded around to buy the turves; and how she sold in bulk to the prosperous, but broke the loads down into small quantities costing a few pence for the poor. The recorded how one poor woman at Ashburton, who took in washing, was always waiting anxiously for her on delivery day. She would take the peat, use it for the washing, collect the washing-money in mid-afternoon and then pay for the peat at the end of the day.

According to William Crossing, many sellers of peat loaded their donkeys to a point of peat-bearing extremity and a strong animal would be in great demand. Crossing tells of James Stephens ('Uncle Jimmy'), of Mary Tavy, who had a donkey that actually seemed to like the task and, when it and Uncle Jimmy's pony were waiting to be loaded, *'insisted on being loaded first, and should his master, or any of the labourers who might be present, commence giving either of their ponies their burden before he was attended to he would resent it, or to use the words of the old man, "he would get in a proper tear", and was only to be appeased by the immediate piling of his own load'*.

In the early 1880s it was discovered that naphtha cold be produced by processing peat. Naphtha, an inflammable oil, or gas, was used for lamps and primitive heating.

In 1846, following an abortive attempt to produce naphtha at Bachelors' Hall, Peter Adams and Jacob Hall Drew founded the British Patent Naphtha Company and took over part of Dartmoor prison. They extracted naphtha and oils from the peat and produced candles and crude gas. This entailed laying a tramway and installing equipment. The total capital cost was £19,000.

By 1847 they had treated 8,200 tons of peat. However, the enterprise had fallen far short of its expectations and the naphtha initiative foundered.

Other naphtha undertakings were established in the south of Dartmoor, but the smoky and generally unacceptable characteristics of the fuel meant that the other 'factories' followed Princetown into the hands of the liquidators.

At the turn of the century there was one last attempt to revive the popularity of peat, but other than in times of coal scarcity, it has never enjoyed a recovery despite the creation of various entrepreneurial bodies like the West of England Compressed Peat Company which opened a railway link-line into the main London

DARTMOOR WILDERNESS… The bleak landscape hid wealth of a sort for those who could exploit it.

and South Western Railway route at Bridestowe station, designed to carry Dartmoor peat to the hearths of Britain.

Britain discovered, as Dartmoor housewives already knew, that although peat – if added to a fire of crackling furze – would make a homely warm and aromatic fire, the quantity of ash left behind made it highly unsuited as a fuel for a conventional grate.

Dartmoor boasted one other industry sharing 'p' with peat – Powder.

No, not the cosmetic power for ladies' complexions, but the powder mills associated with the 'black-powder' used as explosives in the quarrying industry. One of the more interesting people associated with this was Mr George Frean, who opened the powder mills at Postbridge, in 1844.

As befits a man who lived by the means of demolition, George Frean also had more delicate and less violent interests.

A tribute paid to him on his death in 1868, referred to his much wider contribution to the development and improvement of Dartmoor and, incidentally, recalled that he had been personally commended by Prince Albert.

According to the *Western Morning News: 'He was a man of great enterprise, and sank large sums of money on the Crown property on the Moor, which he rented.'*

In the late 1850s, ice works were established on the common above the little village of Sourton, but operations did not last long. The collecting of lichens from the rocks of Dartmoor, and which were used for making a dye, at one time almost assumed the character of an industry. Women and children were employed in the task and were able to earn about two shillings (10p) a day. People were appointed to receive the moss, which was sent to Plymouth for exportation, and formed a profitable article of commerce.

The Prison on the Moor

WITHOUT the benefit of any proof whatsoever, it became so-called 'common knowledge' during the dark days of the second world war that the 'Personal' columns of our great national newspapers were crammed with brief, cryptic messages that either acted as a point of liaison for secret agents and spies, or assuming that even *The Times* could penetrate occupied Europe, reassured the underground that an escaper had safely returned home.

All pretty fanciful. But was it? And was there not, therefore, the possibility of a hidden message in the innocent-looking post card that reached Mr and Mrs E Couteux, of Rocquaine, St Peters, Guernsey, on 22 February 1927?

It was from 'Ernie'. He'd been somewhere where it had been pouring with rain. But he didn't say where.

What he did say, however, was that he had 'enjoyed my stay' and was 'leaving tonight for Paris'.

But 'Ernie' made an obvious mistake that blew his cover! On the front of the post card was a picture of Dartmoor Prison. So that's where he'd been; that's where it had poured with rain; and that's why he was wasting no time in getting to Paris.

It could be argued that this is too devious and fictionally flawed a way of introducing a picture of Dartmoor Prison. Yes, perhaps it is, but the 'Prison on the Moor' has had many stranger experiences in almost two centuries of existence. Men have been murdered whilst inside its walls. There have been mutinies and riots. It has held Frenchmen and Americans as prisoners-of-war, and conscientious objectors incarcerated for their beliefs. One prisoner used it as bed and breakfast accommodation as he visited neighbouring towns

THE PRISON… This picture of the jail was sent in 1927 to an address in Guernsey.

and villages to meet his friends. And, on at least one occasion, men have broken in by climbing its walls in a desperate bid to help a would-be escaper.

Against that true background, 'Ernie's' created story becomes more credible.

The creation of the 'Prison on the Moor' began in 1785 with the appointment of Mr (later, Sir) Thomas Tyrwhitt as Lord Warden of the Stannaries. In this grand-sounding role he had the duty of administering and developing Crown interests on Dartmoor. In that year he literally dug the first sod of profitable Crown involvement by enclosing a sheltered spot of land and creating a farm at Tor Royal, a short distance from what is now Princetown.

Answering directly to the then Prince of Wales, he experimented with the growing of flax and hemp and in the use of lime. From the vicinity of Tor Royal he built a rough track to link into the main road from Tavistock to Moretonhampstead, at Two Bridges.

He built homes for farm workers, a mill and an inn which he called *The Plume of Feathers* after the Prince of Wales' distinctive emblem. He combined houses, mill and pub into a small settle-

64

ment which he called 'Prince's Town' after his royal master.

By 1803, as forecast by those better experienced in the nature and character of the Moor, the whole dream had collapsed, leaving a disused road, empty homes, a tollgate at which nobody paid, and a pub with no customers. Tyrwhitt's dream had become Tyrwhitt's folly.

The war with France provided a new avenue for his ingenuity.

There were so many prisoners-of-war that even civilian prisons were creaking at the seams. Old warships were pressed into service as prison hulks and Tyrwhitt discovered that each of the six hulks moored of Plymouth cost £3,000 a year in food, water, supervision and medical bills to offset the squalid conditions.

Tyrwhitt waged a successful campaign to have a prison built at Prince's Town, arguing that there was plenty of granite available; no shortage of water and healthy work; and a good road link, via the accommodation track he had built twenty years earlier.

His persistence paid off and, in 1805, approval was given to his plan to build five prison blocks, each accommodating one thousand

PRINCETOWN… Hard at work in the prison quarry.

THE JAIL… An officer patrols while convicts construct prison buildings – a picture from 1880.

men. There would be a hospital and accommodation for five-hundred officers and soldiers who would act as guards. The total cost would be in the region of £70,000, he estimated.

Work began in the winter of 1805. The conditions were cold and wet and the masons, drafted in from Cornwall, demanded more money if they were to work throughout the bitter weather. In one week alone, 'the eligible healthy' site of the prison had become so unbearable that the contractors met a setback to the tune of £120 in lost working time.

The deadline for the opening, in September 1807, came and went. Work had progressed merely to a basic level of clearing the site, laying the foundations, and carting vast quantities of stone.

Pressure was applied on the workmen. They, for their part, rebelled with shoddy work. Walls fell down shortly after being built; floors became dangerously uneven; steps crumbled. The opening was finally postponed to 24 May 1809.

When the first contingent of French prisoners marched in, under escort, from Plymouth, costs had already soared to over £74,000.

Tyrwhitt himself thrived. He was MP for Plymouth from 1806

until, in 1812, he was appointed Gentleman Usher of the Black Rod. He died on 24 February 1833 at the age of 71. A memorial tablet to the man who, despite his mistakes and misjudgements, was still regarded as *'this unwearied worker for the welfare of the Moor'*, was placed in Princetown church recalling that his *'name and memory are inseparable from all the great works on Dartmoor, and cannot cease to be honoured in this district'.*

Diplomatically overlooked in the eulogy was the fact that the final cost of his £70,000 prison would be £130,000 and that, far from providing modest comfort for five thousand prisoners-of-war, it would have to accommodate as many as nine thousand at certain times.

The French were very popular 'guests'. They neither sought nor caused trouble. They had a definite class structure. Officers receiving money paid other prisoners to clean and cook for them. They were known as 'Les Lords'. A second tier of prison society was 'Les Labourers', they made goods – sometimes out of bone – for sale locally. Then there were 'Les Indifferents', the idle; 'Les Minables', who gambled; and 'Les Romains' – the poor and failed gamblers who had pledged their all in expectation yet would live on low rations and with little clothing in the squalid reality of debt.

By 1811, Trywhitt's vision had become a working reality. The historian, Tristram Risdon, wrote of it as *'probably the finest prison of its kind. The outer wall encloses a circle of about thirty acres. Within this is another wall which encloses the area in which the prison stands ... the country people are admitted, who resort to a daily market with vegetables and such other things as the prisoners purchase to add to the fare that is provided for them and which they buy at lower rates than they could generally be procured for at the market towns.'*

In April 1813, the French prisoners-of-war were joined by American military prisoners. Unlike the French the Americans were virtually paupers who, ignored by their own government, had no cash which to buy the tobacco that was so necessary to their way of life. They bickered amongst themselves, stole and were violent.

To offset the hardship of the winter of 1813, the American government introduced a small cash allowance for its captured servicemen. This triggered gambling on a massive scale. The total allowance for all the American prisoners amounted to £2,000 per month. Most of it was immediately recycled in gambling and smoking.

In 1814, with the fall of Napoleon Bonaparte, the French left Princetown ... and trouble brewed amongst the frustrated and bored Americans. In April 1815, the tension already mounting, the prisoners were issued with hard biscuit instead of bread. They protested and a sentry over-reacted, sending an American flying with a blow from his musket butt. The Americans stormed the store-house demanding fresh bread. British officers gave way. Bread was issued. An uneasy peace was restored.

Next day there was a further incident in which a sentry refused to return a ball accidentally kicked out of reach of the Americans. They asked for it back – to no avail. They said that if it was not returned, they would climb the wall and get it. They were ignored. An alarm bell rang. Prisoners who had taken part in the incident thought it was the muster signal and that there was a fire. In a large group they ran to their fire point. It was thought that they were gathering for a riot.

They were told to disperse. They did not. Soldiers fixed bayonets. Some demonstrators broke away, others confronted their captors.

A warning volley was fired over their heads, followed by an outbreak of indiscriminate shooting as British soldiers vented their spite and frustration on their foes.

In less than five minutes it was all over, and nine Americans were on their way to unmarked graves and more than fifty to the hospital.

The true irony of the horror did not occur for another two weeks when a peace treaty was signed and the repatriation of the Americans began. And there was a further irony in that, the peace that followed the conflict with Napoleon had ended and Britain was again at war with France. As the Americans marched out, the first of the second phase of French prisoners of war were marching in!

Peace with France dawned again, after just 100 days.

The prisoners were released and, in 1816, the establishment was decommissioned as a war prison.

The effect of closure on Princetown itself was both dramatic and

MUTINY... The aftermath of the 1932 mutiny, the offices destroyed and ransacked.

immediate. For several years the French had kept a buoyant (though dubious) economy alive. Many of them had received prize money from their own country; and others reputedly turned out forged Bank of England banknotes in the privacy of their cells and passed them off in the prison market on unsuspecting local traders!

It was at this stage that Sir Thomas Tyrwhitt re-emerged in the role of good fairy.

Although what he proposed would take until 1850 to materialise, he campaigned and argued successfully that his great prison could become a civilian one. By then Australia and the other penal colonies had refused to take any more British convicts. Transportation was at an end and so the establishment, renamed 'Her Majesty's Prison Dartmoor', opened its gates to its first one-hundred-and-fifty criminal inmates after the abandoned and dilapidated original accommodation had been refurbished.

For more that fifty years, convicts and civilian craftsmen and labourers worked together to provide accommodation in 1908 for its target of thirteen hundred inmates.

The new regime was one of contradiction. Although men were treated harshly with mental and physical brutality, the prison diet was so good that Princetown residents called at the prison for bread and other left overs.

For a variety of offences ranging from 'murderous assault' to idleness or refusal to work, a convict could be put on bread and water, flogged with a cat o' nine tails with between twenty-four and thirty-six lashes, or restrained by either a strait-jacket or ball and chain, leg-irons and manacles.

Minor riots and disturbances were commonplace as Dartmoor Prison had become the home of violent criminals serving sentences of such length and severity that discipline or punishment held no dread.

In 1928 the first prisoner to escape by motor car made his exit. In 1931 bloodhounds were used to track escapers for the first time. Dartmoor Prison, it seemed, was never out of the news with its sinister reputation of being 'Half-way to Hell, the purgatory of lost, forgotten, lonely and tormented souls'.

January 1932 saw, arguably, the blackest milestone in the prison's history – the famous mutiny in which more than one hundred desperate convicts went on the rampage, soon to be joined by countless colleagues. In his book *Dartmoor Prison*, Rufus Endle, who was then a local reporter, wrote of what he saw that day: 'The mutineers had positioned themselves behind a stone wall on top of which was their ringleader, or one of them. The police were met with a fusillade of stones, coal, pick-handles and other weapons, but their well-wielded truncheons soon caused the more timid to run for shelter and the deserted diehards gave up. It was all over in twenty minutes but it took two hours to round them all up, strip them and lock them up.

'Plymouth fire brigade arrived and when the outer doors were opened to admit it had a split-second glimpse of a free-for-all, of bodies lying prone on the ground and a holocaust of flames soaring up in the background'.

There was widespread damage to the administrative block; the prison fire engine was wrecked; and the prison officers' mess was looted.

A terse Home Office press release told the news media: *'About two hundred convicts out of four hundred broke away and caused damage. No convict escaped and no officer of the prison or the police was seriously injured. Many convicts are in prison more or less seriously wounded, some with gunshot wounds but more as the result of the baton charge by the police. About twenty prisoners received minor injuries'.*

The statement underestimated the casualties. It was later admitted that twenty-three prisoners suffered from baton wounds; that seven were shot, one of whom died later; that four officers were seriously injured in the mutiny, and that twenty others were less seriously injured.

Thirty prisoners were sent for trial on charges of causing a riot; of damaging of destroying public property; and of assault. They received combined sentences totalling just under one hundred years.

Merrivale Bridge. Near Princetown.

MERRIVALE BRIDGE… Pictured in traffic-free days. Now Merrivale is a favourite stop for tourists on their way to look at Dartmoor Prison just up the road.

Animals, Potatoes and Stone

THE obvious is often so obvious that it needs re-stating if it's not to be overlooked.

For that reason it's worth recalling that cattle, sheep, ponies and rabbits are amongst the main animal dwellers of Dartmoor, with quarrying and the working and mining of materials amongst the key money-generators which, in their day, turned a substance of nature into a profitable commodity.

Sheep, it's said, have always been Dartmoor's most important animal – even more useful than man.

The reason is simple. As an animal they are virtually self-sufficient with a high survival rate. As a crop they have the double virtue of providing wool as well as flesh, so they have always had a high relative value status.

Anyone who knows the Moor will say that the Dartmoor sheep (most likely, actually, to be of the Scotch breed), is not the stupid creature that humans believe it to be. Stories are told of sheep going up to a cattle-grid that frustrates other animals and of actually wriggling their way across. Similarly, the best way of testing whether or not the walls on a sheep enclosure are high enough was to imprison one sheep. Within a remarkably short space of time, the captive animal would either jump or butt its way to freedom, thus identifying the weakest point.

In 1793 it was decided, for the first time, to try to carry out a sheep census. Despite the wisdom of the dry old farmer who suggested that the most accurate way would be to count the number of legs and divide by four, it was decided that it would be possible to get a rough idea by physically counting at key points.

When the task was completed, the figures revealed a sheep population of between one-hundred-and-ten-thousand and one-hundred-and-twenty-thousand animals grazing the Moor.

A follow-up count four years later found that the numbers had fallen to about eighty-thousand. The cause, it was said, was that the so-called 'improvers of Dartmoor' had pinched the best of the Moor for cattle and crops.

Second only to Northumberland for sheep-farming, Dartmoor, was noted in 1806 as having, in August and September of that year, *'flocks more numerous on the Moor, and in much higher condition, than on any similar pasture grounds in England ... and yet the grass in the beginning of November was scarcely half consumed'.*

One of the most effective ways of carrying out a pony census was what became known as a 'drift' whereby, on a date fixed by the Duchy of Cornwall, as well as the surrounding commoners, the animals were counted by men summoned by the blowing of horns on the tors early on the morning of the count. The point at which the horns were blown became known as 'blowing stones'. These stones were carefully selected and placed so that there was a cavity in one side. By directing the horn into this, the sound was amplified. 'Drifters' drove the animals in front of them to a collection-point, shouting and using dogs. At the census-point, owners could claim their animals. Any not claimed would then be impounded until their owners were able to repossess them after paying their grazing fees, together with the costs of watering the livestock.

One drive, in the 1860s, was witnessed by a Mr W F Collier who wrote that: *'all the ponies or colts are driven from every nook and corner by men on foot, one horseback, and with dogs, to Merrivale Bridge. It is a curious site to see herds of fleet and sure-footed little animals, in a great state of alarm at the unusual uproar or hooting, holloaing, and horns sounding, galloping over the More all in one direction, giving their tails and manes to the wind. The movement of ponies on the tors and the noise proclaim to drift to all the world ... an officer of the Duchy stands upon a stone and reads a formidable document with seals attached to it to the assembly'.*

Historically the Dartmoor pony is the oldest animal-dweller, well-known for its ruggedness and strength. They have served as pack-horses carrying unbelievably massive burdens sure-footedly

EMBLEM OF THE MOOR... The Dartmoor pony has been adopted by the National Park as its emblem, but fewer farmers now keep the sturdy little animals because of the problems of winter feeding and the dangers of traffic.

across the most treacherous stretches of the Moor, as well as having worked in the coal mines of Wales and other parts of Britain. Hardiness is born into them. In their natural habitat they know no shelter except what may be provided by an obliging boulder or a hedge. They are strangers to hay and other formal fodder and can, in blizzard times, go five days without food. With an uncanny knack they will, when the Moor is hidden by snow, remember where the best heather is to be found and, scraping the snow aside, will browse contentedly.

They rarely move far from where they were born, preferring to congregate in small 'family' groups. Nowadays they are in great demand as riding-ponies for children. Their popularity lies in that they are cheap and 'natural' despite the fact that they should be black and shaggy, rather than the much-sought black-and-white mongrel that has been increasingly introduced in response to consumer taste.

Dartmoor cattle love the short grass that abounds on the Moor. Like the ponies, they tend to be unadventurous and rarely stray far from familiar areas.

Dartmoor's warrens carry a link – through rabbits – backwards in times to the days when they were introduced by the Normans for sporting purposes. Although, traditionally, the Normans regarded warrens as being land set aside for the rearing of all game, including hare, pheasant and partridge, in the case of Dartmoor, the warrens were exclusively associated with rabbits.

Sir Walter Raleigh is reputed as having introduced the potato to Britain. It thrived in all temperate and sub-tropical regions and on the north-eastern quarter of Dartmoor where it often needed the encouragement of specialist treatment and manures.

Farmers would sometimes enter into an agreement with manufacturers to offer 'public testimony and endorsement' of the product in exchange for generous discounts or other 'recognitions'.

Around 1900, Mr Joe Endacott posed for the standard picture taken by the manufacturers. Although the caption put it, rather formally, that: *'Mr Endacott says – "I may say that I have been a user of your Special Potato Manure for some years, and am very well pleased with it".'*, the simple message that went with Hadfield's Special Potato Manure was: *'if it's good enough for Joe Endacott, then it must be pretty good'.*

Mr. ENDACOTT says—I 'may say that I have been a user of your SPECIAL POTATO MANURE for some years, and am very well pleased with it.

Mr Endacott posed with two of his workers (and a dog), together with Hadfield's representative.

A keen and cynical eye might, perhaps, have noted that the potatoes were carefully piled to emphasise the large ones at the top rather than the smaller ones at the bottom of the display.

However, Dartmoor potatoes were eagerly bought locally as well as being sent by rail to places like Covent Garden, Manchester and Birmingham, the main crop being dug from September through to the end of November, providing a ready demand for locally-based casual workers. It was heavy work, not the least when each filled basket – weighing some fifty-six pounds – had to be moved or lifted up onto a cart.

As in Cornwall, mining was once a traditional industry of the Moor.

Long before cattle, sheep, ponies and crops became a commercial proposition, Dartmoor folk toiled in the mines. As an industry it had its peaks and troughs, eventually fading away towards the end of the nineteenth century. There were workings for tin, for copper and for lead, mostly in and around Mary Tavy where there are still visible reminders in the stately chimneys and the solid and sedate ruined engine houses. In the 1870s a mine was opened on the site of old workings near Hexworthy, but failed after a few years.

The lot of the miner was never a happy one. The job was wet, it was dirty, it was difficult and it was dangerous … all for poor financial return and the likelihood of early death through accident or ailment. Since the basic pay was low and the real rewards lay with productivity, men worked long hours and took incredible risks.

In the days of King Charles, Thomas Westcote visited several Dartmoor mines. The miners, he found, lived off rough bread and dry cheese; they drank from streams; they lived in the shelter of clusters of stones. What Westcote wrote, over three hundred years ago, was not to change for the remaining two centuries of Dartmoor mining: *'No labourer whatsoever undergoes greater hazard or peril or danger, nor in hard and coarse diet doth equal him"*.

Dartmoor's last working mine, Hen Roose, survived until 1916 although a couple of small enterprises re-working the discarded 'tailings' of other mines remained active until 1939.

THE MOOR from HAY TOR 13406

THE FACE OF THE MOOR… The intractable moorland rock is every-where. It is still quarried for building and roadstone.

As mining died, so quarrying moved into a new and greater importance. Granite was needed for building great enterprises like Dartmoor Prison. It went into houses and pubs, roads and railways. It was sent miles overland to where it was needed for ports and harbours, for proud municipal offices. It was stacked in vast columns for railway viaducts and bridges. It graced churches and cathedrals.

Teams of powerful horses hauled huge blocks of granite to where it could be loaded onto rail-waggons. Quarrying became a prison activity with some convict teams cutting, facing the stone and using it to build solid additions to the gaol.

The area from Merrivale to the outskirts of Princetown tells of 'living' and 'dead' quarrying, with its vivid contrast between modern-day extraction and the ghost settlements where once the quarrymen lived in tiny houses with small gardens; sent their children to the quarry school and worshipped in the quarry chapel.

The railways created an insatiable demand for stone in another form – smaller pieces for the ballast that would be packed beneath the rails to give a solid cushion against vibration.

One of the great ballast-producing quarries is Meldon, a few miles from Okehampton. Up to the outbreak of the 1939-45 war, the management and workers kept up the tradition of having a special lunch at Christmas when, after the meal, the whole work-force had to trail outside for their annual photograph to be taken, usually squeezed into the narrow space between the quarry face and the railway line which carried the stone away from the working area. At its prime, the quarry employed over two-hundred workers. Nowadays, with mechanisation and improved efficiency, it achieves higher yields with but one eighth of the original number of quarrymen.

Not only was Meldon a large employer, but it justified a large neighbouring hamlet where its workers lived. Although there have always been other quarries in the neighbourhood, Meldon has always been the largest and has always been owned either by the pre-nationalisation private railway companies, or, since, by British Rail.

Okehampton

WILLIAM Crossing wrote, in 1900: '*A new danger threatens the Commoners. Certain sounds are in the air very disquieting to those who love Dartmoor for its charm of solitude and its old-world customs, and who value their ancient rights. The Military Manoeuvres Bill lately before Parliament contained proposals that would sadly interfere with the exercise of the latter, and by which the great lone land would be shorn of much of its attractiveness. The Commoner – the man of Devon – will yield to none in patriotism, and will be ready to make a sacrifice if the needs of the country demand it, but he is surely entitled to more consideration than he would receive if the contemplated measure were to become law*'.

Fifty years later, Dr W G Hoskins was to write: '*The passing years see ever-growing encroachments by military and other Service Departments upon the available land … The military have had a grip on the Northern part of the Moor, near Okehampton, for the last fifty years or so, but have now extended their firing activities over a much wider area …, with their unfailing instinct for choosing beautiful places to wreck*'.

But was it to be an insensitive sadistic rape of the Moor with little thought to effect, and even less attention to, at least, economic compensation?

Perhaps the view of Vian Smith, expressed in 1966, holds the balance: '*My observation is that those who are quick with disgruntled comments in peace are among the first to expect professional efficiency in times of emergency. To expect efficiency without conceding the need for training is illogical. Military training over so wide an area is a nuisance; occasionally dangerous to individuals who do not observe or understand the regulations. But there are worse offences than committing a nuisance. Committing to foreign service young soldiers who have not been thoroughly trained is*

OKEHAMPTON... Poppy sellers in 1928.

one of them'.

Soldiers of the Royal Horse Artillery trained for the fields of Flanders at Okehampton Battle Camp before the 1914-18 war, unaware of the anachronistic conflict that lay ahead – field-guns versus long-range heavy artillery, horses against tanks, clean-shaven young Englishmen inhaling deadly German gas.

For Okehampton, military training had already become an annual ritual of spectacle and excitement in which, for a few weeks, the permanent camp buildings would be massively outnumbered by bivouacs and supply tents, and the Moor would echo to the jingle of harness, the sound of metalled wheels on roads, the sweaty smell of horses and the endless sounds of rehearsed battle.

The soldiers meant money for traders in the town, and ceremonial spectacle for the townspeople.

Dartmoor had been used for military training since the days of the Napoleonic wars, but permanent camps were not thought of until the 1870s, when the concept was floated by the War Office that it would be convenient to take out a nine-hundred-and-ninety-nine year lease. To sweeten local opinion, it was laid down that all fodder, victuals and supplies should be purchased locally, thus making a dramatic input to the economy of the immediate area. On the other hand, it was conceded that this would do little more than offset the money lost to tourism as a consequence of a military presence, it being appreciated that any would-be holidaymaker might think twice if they looked at a map of the area and saw large sections marked off as firing ranges.

To balance this thinking, it was suggested that restricted public access could have a beneficial effect on establishing some localities as nature reserves, while the provision of military roads might even open up the Moor to tourists at non-training times.

The 1920s brought change.

When the soldiers returned, it was with tractors instead of horses and with bigger pieces of artillery than had been seen before. It was said that there was more horsepower and mechanisation at the Okehampton Battle Camp than the surrounding towns and villages could muster between them. The war had left its mark and Okehampton adopted a warmly paternalistic pride towards its military visitors.

BATTLE CAMP... The horse artillery above Okehampton on manoeuvres before the first world war.

The troops responded, with an immense show of ceremony.

When units still using horses arrived, they occupied the sidings at Okehampton railway station, with the soldiers and horses travelling in the same sort of rolling stock. But, after a short period of grooming and smartening up, the unit would appear fully-equipped and in dress uniform as if for a major ceremonial occasion, parading through the town before making its way to camp. This had an unexpected side effect of making the Okehampton district a major recruitment area for horse and artillery units, whereas most other would-be soldiers tended to apply for an infantryman's role in the Devonshire Regiment. Certainly the local skills of horsemanship made the area a fruitful enlistment point for the Royal Horse Artillery.

Of course, a consequence of links with the Army had made Okehampton bear a high price in dead and disabled men through the Great War.

Armistice Day, when at the eleventh day of the eleventh month, a whole nation came to a silent halt for two minutes' silence, was loyally supported by people of all ages and all social classes from toddlers and Boy Scouts to country wives and the well-to-do. In the 1920s the poppies were only sold on the day before Armistice Day, not for weeks in advance. Although the collectors were united under the reminder: 'If ye break faith with us who die, we shall not sleep though poppies grow in Flanders', the size of the donation dictated the size of the poppy that could be proudly worn next day.

Another unexpected link between Okehampton and the Army was that the regular visits to camp, of top military bands created a tradition of bandsmen and brass and silver bands. Although it was a small community, it boasted three major bands in the decade leading to the 1939-45 war. In 1927, the Town Band was given the premier title of Okehampton Borough Band, under its bandmaster, James Gale. However, in 1934, he broke away to form the Okehampton Brass Band. This was eventually overshadowed by the third band – the Okehampton Excelsior Silver Band – in a town that always had been and still is, very musical and influenced by self-made entertainment. The late Bob Cann, a famous Dartmoor folk musician, learned his craft in the 1920s when he was

ON PARADE... A picture from the 1920s.

84

Fore Street, Okehampton.

OKEHAMPTON... The town's main street before motor traffic.

only about five years old. In his reminiscences he said that he picked up many of the tunes from military marches, thus confirming the link between military musical example and the adaptive ability of local musicians.

Like most towns, Okehampton could boast a great personal benefactor. In their case it was Sidney Simmons, who teed-off for the opening of Okehampton golf links, in July 1913.

He was born in the town in 1842 in one of the cottages that lies in the courtyard of what is now the Museum of Dartmoor Life. Although his parents ran a printing business, Sidney served his apprenticeship in a Plymouth drapery before going to London to join the staff of a carpet manufacturer, eventually becoming their sales manager for North America.

He travelled the world and, whilst overseas, came across a carpet-cleaning machine. He brought it back to Finchley, developed and patented it, and made his fortune.

He never forgot his native town and frequently returned to give it various gifts. He bought and restored Okehampton Castle before donating it to the borough; he built and supported almshouses; and he acquired and laid out what was to become the main leisure area, Simmons Park, opened in 1907. He presented a bowling green and inspired, partly financed and was closely associated with the golf links.

Despite his love of his native town, he did not return there to live in retirement but died, and was buried, in Finchley.

THE LINKS… Sydney Simmons tees off at the opening of the golf links in July 1913.

BALL HILL… The town always had a strong community spirit – here is the volunteer fire brigade in action on Ball Hill about 1926. Gorse fires were common then, as now.

THE BAND… Okehampton Borough Band at the Agricultural Show in the early 1930s. The Town Band was renamed the Borough Band in 1927. James Gale remained bandmaster and can be seen to the right of the centre pole of the stand. In 1934, however, he broke away and formed his own rival Okehampton Brass Band.

Well Worth the Climb!

DARTMOOR is not promiscuous. When it gives itself, it has demanded a rigorous winning. It has never regarded itself as being there for the taking, but has to be earned.

Empty words?

Well, just apply them to Brentor. Once conquered, it offers an unequalled view ... but conquering it is not for the lazy as it entails a tough walk up a steep tor. But the reward more than justifies the effort.

Standing some thirteen hundred feet above sea level, legend links it closely to the sea that can be seen in the distance. Admittedly, it's not an exclusive story.

According to tradition, a rich merchant drowning at sea vowed that, were he to be saved, he would build a church on the first piece of land he could sea. Thus Brentor, almost twenty miles from the open sea 'won' its church. It seems that the merchant either had a sight-defect or else was selective to have overlooked equally prominent outcrops between Brentor and Plymouth Sound!

A more colourful explanation is that the Devil decided to make things a little tough for local Christians and so, to test their enthusiasm, he pinched stones from a church being built in the valley below, and carried them to the top. The Christians argued that if the Devil was daft enough to take the stones to so commanding a peak, they would let him do the carrying and they would finish the job.

The truth is that the stones were taken to the top on the protesting backs of workers from Tavistock Abbey when the decision was taken to build a series of preaching stations in the neighbourhood.

The task was probably undertaken in the days of Bishop Bronescombe, bishop of Exeter, in or around 1268, improving a site first developed as the shrine of 'St Michael of the Rock' built by Robert Giffard in about 1140.

Presumably on the assumption that, once you'd reached the top, it was better to stay where you were for a while rather than go to and fro, the Abbey authorities gave it a three-day fair on the eve of St Michael's day, the saint's day itself, and the morning after – on 28, 29 and 30 September each year.

When Tavistock Abbey was dissolved, St Michael's Brentor, passed to the Russell family before they took over their full major land-owning role of Tavistock and its environs.

The present church was reopened in 1890 after extensive repairs. It is regarded as being 'as stout as a fortress' despite its minute size, being only five meters wide and twelve metres long, with a tower standing some thirteen metres.

If, indeed, there is a Christian lighthouse on Dartmoor, then St Michael's Brentor answers just such a requirement, being an unmistakable landmark of faith and visibility from many miles away, and even from Cornwall.

According to Tristram Risdon: *'It is a church, full bleak, and weather beaten, all alone as it were forsaken, whose churchyard doth hardly afford depth of earth to bury the dead; yet doubtless they rest there as in sumptuous St Peters, until the day of doom'.*

ACKNOWLEDGEMENTS

THE AUTHOR would like to express his warmest thanks to Alan Endacott, of the Museum of Dartmoor life, Okehampton, and to David German, of Princetown, for their wonderful help and kindness in providing some of the illustrations for this book.

Not only did they provide pictures, but the wealth of local lore – and expert knowledge – discharged by both of them left the author (for once in his life!) admitting to a feeling of total inadequacy.

BOOKS CONSULTED

Alford, Rev D.P.
THE ABBOTS OF TAVISTOCK   W. Brendon & Son.

Baring-Gould, Rev Sabine
A BOOK OF DARTMOOR   Bodley Head

Burton, S.H.
DEVON VILLAGES   Robert Hale

CHAMBERS BIOGRAPHICAL DICTIONARY   W. & R. Chambers

Crossing, William
ONE HUNDRED YEARS ON DARTMOOR   Western Morning News

Endle, Rufus
DARTMOOR PRISON   Bossiney Books

Fiennes, Celia
DIARIES AND TRAVELS

Gunnell, Clive
MY DARTMOOR   Bossiney Books

Hoskins, W.G.
DEVON   Collins

Hunt, Robert
POPULAR ROMANCES OF THE WEST OF ENGLAND
Chatto & Windus

Morgan, Eileen
SIR BEVILLE GRENVILLE OF STOWE   Arthur H. Stockwell

Murray, John
MURRAY'S HANDBOOK FOR DEVON AND CORNWALL, 1859
David & Charles

Penny, A.D.V.
KELLY COLLEGE REGISTER 1877 – 1927   Tavistock Printing Co.

Pettit, Paul
SHELL GUIDE TO DEVON, CORNWALL & THE ISLES OF SCILLY
Michael Joseph

Rowe, Rev. Samuel A.
A PERAMBULATION OF DARTMOOR   Devon Books

Thomas, David St John
REGIONAL HISTORY OF THE RAILWAYS OF GREAT BRITAIN
Phoenix House

MORE BOSSINEY BOOKS...

SUPERSTITION AND FOLKLORE
by Michael Williams. 44 photographs.
A survey of Westcountry Superstitions: Interviews on the subject and some Cornish and Devon folklore.
'...the strictures that we all ignore at our peril. To help us to keep out of trouble, Mr Williams has prepared a comprehensive list.'
Frank Kempe, North Devon Journal-Herald

STRANGE STORIES FROM DEVON
by Rosemary Anne Lauder & Michael Williams. 45 photographs.
Strange shapes and places, strange characters, the man they couldn't hang, and a Salcombe mystery, the Lynmouth disaster and a mysterious house are some of the strange stories from Devon.
'...full of good stories, accompanied by many photographs of local happenings which have mystified.'
Mary Richards, Tavistock Times

LEGENDS OF DEVON
by Sally Jones
Devon is a mine of folklore and myth. Here is a journey through legendary Devon. Sally Jones brings into focus some fascinating tales, showing us that the line dividing fact and legend is an intriguing one.
'Sally Jones has trodden the path of legendary Devon well...'
Tavistock Times

MYSTERIES OF THE SOUTH WEST
by Tamsin Thomas of BBC Radio Cornwall
A tour of ancient sites in Cornwall and on Dartmoor.
'There is little doubt that Tamsin Thomas has become the 'Voice of Cornwall'.
Ronnie Hoyle, North Cornwall Advertiser

AROUND AND ABOUT THE FAL
by David Mudd
A rich tapestry of a famous Cornish river and its people.

THE CRUEL CORNISH SEA
by David Mudd
Cornish shipwrecks spanning 400 years.

DEVON REFLECTIONS
by Jilly Carter
In her years with TSW, Jilly Carter travelled thousands of miles for news stories and interviews, She now uses that knowledge – and affection for Devon – in producing a balanced portrait of the county.

SUPERNATURAL INVESTIGATION
by Michael Williams
'...has to be the one you read in front of a roaring fire, curtains closed against the howling gale and a stiff whisky within arm's reach to calm the nerves.'

Wendy Hanwell, Tavistock Times

DEVON CURIOSITIES
Jane Langton

DART – THE MAGICAL RIVER
Ken Duxbury

GHOSTS OF DEVON
Peter Underwood

GHOSTS & PHANTOMS OF THE WEST
Peter Underwood

CASTLES OF DEVON
James Mildren

We shall be pleased to send you our catalogue giving full details of our growing list of titles for Devon, Cornwall, Dorset and Somerset as well as forthcoming publications. If you have difficulty in obtaining our titles, write direct to Bossiney Books, Land's End, St Teath, Bodmin, Cornwall.